BULLY B.E.A.N.S.

Activity and Idea Book

published by

National Center for Youth Issues
Practical Guidance Resources
Educators Can Trust
ncyi.org

What Can You Make Of It?

How many words (two or more letters) can you make from the phrase:
BULLIES EVERYWHERE ARE NOW STOPPED!

Write your answers below. Use the back of the paper if you run out of room.

1. _____

2. _____

3. _____

4. _____

5. _____

6. _____

7. _____

8. _____

9. _____

10. _____

11. _____

12. _____

13. _____

14. _____

15. _____

16. _____

17. _____

18. _____

19. _____

20. _____

21. _____

22. _____

Think About What You SAY!

Write down ten mean and hurtful things that you have said to others:

1. _____
2. _____
3. _____
4. _____
5. _____
6. _____
7. _____
8. _____
9. _____
10. _____

Circle the meanest thing above that you have said to someone else.

Why did you say it?

_____
_____
_____

How did you feel after you said it?

_____
_____
_____

How do you think your words made the person feel?

_____
_____
_____

What could you have done differently?

_____
_____

Think About What You HEAR!

Write down ten mean and hurtful things that you have heard others say to you:

1. _____
2. _____
3. _____
4. _____
5. _____
6. _____
7. _____
8. _____
9. _____
10. _____

Circle the meanest thing said to you above.

Why do you think the person said it?

_____
_____
_____

How did you feel after they said it?

_____
_____
_____

How do you think the person that said it felt?

_____
_____
_____

What could that person have done differently?

_____
_____

Bystander Club T-Shirt

Directions:

You've been accepted as a new member of the Bystander Club. The club president has asked you to design a T-shirt. The purpose of the T-shirt is to teach others how to be a powerful bystander and prevent bullying. Make up your own club logo or slogan that will get this message to across to others.

Picture This

Draw a picture of one powerful, mean bully.

Draw a picture of two or three targets (the people who get picked on).

Draw a picture of 10 bystanders working together to have more power than the bully.

Dear Friend,

Congratulations!

You have just been given a new job.

You are an advice columnist for your local paper, and people write in to you asking for help with their problems. First of all, give yourself a clever pen name (i.e. Happy Maker, Smile Doctor, Dr. Peace etc.) Then, answer the following letters on a seperate sheet of paper:

Dear (Your Pen Name Here) -

Every day when I go to school, I have to deal with Dalton. He thinks he is in charge of everything and everyone! He always kisses up to our teacher and she thinks he's perfect - but he is so mean! He always calls me Geek Face and makes fun of my clothes. Last week, he had a big party at his house and invited everybody in our class but me. He said it would be dangerous for me to be there because the garbage man might come to pick up trash while the party is going on and accidentally mistake me for garbage and take me with him. I have a few friends, but they are only nice to me when Dalton isn't around. I hate coming to school!

Signed - Miserable

Dear (Your Pen Name Here) -

I have a big problem. There is a kid in my class named Dalton who is really mean to other kids. He always gives put-downs and constantly goes out of his way to make certain kids feel bad. Dalton is very smart and he kisses up to our teacher so she thinks he is perfect. Dalton is usually pretty nice to me, but I can't stand the way he treats some of the other kids. He calls them names and makes fun of their clothes. He makes life at school miserable for them. I am afraid to do or say anything to Dalton because I don't want him to start picking on me. I try to be friends with everybody, but I have to be careful about who I hang out with when Dalton is around. What should I do?

Signed - Guilty

Dear (Your Pen Name Here) -

My mom is never home and when she is, she is always on the phone. She seems like she never has time for me. She is so busy with her life and her job that I don't seem to even matter to her. I get more attention from my teacher at school than I do from my own mom. When my mom feels guilty for not spending time with me and my sister (who by the way is very mean to me,) she buys us things and lets us have kids over. Last week, my sister had friends over for a party. She didn't let me near the party. She told me that it would be dangerous for me to come because the garbage man might come to pick up trash while the party is going on and accidentally mistake me for garbage and take me with him. I would rather be at school than at home. At least at school, I can control what happens to me.

Signed - Empty

Challenge!!
Find which letter is written by the following:
- Bystander
- Bully
- Target

SOS, I'm Getting Bullied

Write about a person you know who get's bullied.
- Why do you think this person is being bullied?
- What do others think about this situation?
- What advice would you give this person?

Draw a picture of a person with self-esteem standing up to a bully.

Make your school a "Bully-Free Zone." Conduct a Bully-Free campaign schoolwide that is student generated!!! Make big signs and banners and display them throughout your school. Create stickers for students to wear and stick on their notebooks. Have students read and sign a contract promising to support the Bully-Free Zone Policy.

Mean Eyes

Materials Needed:

• Magazines   • Paper   • Glue

Sometimes people don't even realize it when they are giving you their mean eyes. This activity may teach them what to "look" for!

Look through magazines and cut out 10-15 pair of eyes. Try to get as many different eye expressions as you can. Be careful to only include the eyes, not the mouth or the hair in each picture. Glue the eyes to your paper and write what you think the person is saying or thinking with their eyes underneath each pair. Share your eyes and emotions with the rest of the class. This can be an "eye-opening" experience!!!

Bully Awareness Chart

Purpose: Create bully awareness and teach effective interventions over a period of one month

- After each recess, have students report any and all bullying behaviors that they see either on the playground or inside the school.

- Chart each bullying behavior as they are stated. Make sure that kids do not use any names when reporting. Have them tell what is happening, not who it is happening to.

- Discuss each situation and brainstorm effective interventions that can take place for each bully behavior.

- Repeat this activity for four weeks. At the end of week four, compare your chart for week one with your chart for week four. If your interventions are working, your bully behavior chart should be getting smaller by the week.

Learning From the Past

Interview 10 of your relatives that are grown ups and ask them the following questions:

1. When you were a kid, were you a bully, a target or a bystander?
   _____

2. Can you remember the name of a person who bullied you when you were growing up?
   _____

3. What mean things did the bully do to you and to others?
   _____
   _____

4. What did you do about the bully?
   _____
   _____
   _____

5. How do you feel about the bully today?
   _____
   _____
   _____

6. If you could speak to the bully right now, what would you say to him/her?
   _____
   _____
   _____

Compile and organize your data and present it to the class along with your answers to the following questions:

What is the most interesting thing that you learned by conducting these interviews?

_____
_____
_____

Do you know more about bullying now than your relatives knew when they were young? Explain.

_____
_____
_____

A Cup of Self-Esteem

Materials Needed:

- Glass Pitcher
- Styrofoam cup
- Food coloring
- Water
- Ball Point Pen
- Rubber Garbage Can
- Paper
- Black Permanent Marker

Directions:

- Draw a smiley face on the outside of the Styrofoam cup.
- Pass out a sheet of paper to each student. Have students write 10-15 put-downs (mean things people say to one another) on their papers.
- Fill the glass picture with water and add food coloring. Explain to your students that the colored water represents a person's self esteem.
- Fill the Styrofoam cup full of colored water and hold it over the garbage can. Explain that the full cup represents a person with a great self-esteem.
- Have students start saying the put-downs that they have written down out loud to the cup. Each time a put-down is said aloud, poke a hole in the cup with the pen ruining the happy face on the cup.)
- Watch the self-esteem run out of the cup. This is what can happen to people when they hear put-downs.
- Keep refilling the cup until the pitcher is empty. Self esteem is not like water. We can't just go to the faucet and get more self-esteem. When it's gone, it's gone. It takes a long time for a person to build their self-esteem back up.

Mirror, Mirror On the Wall

Often times, it is very hard to realize when you are a bully.
On a seperate sheet of paper, answer the following questions honestly:

Do others see me as a bully? | Do I see myself as a target? | Am I a bystander?

Do others see me as a bully?

1. Do you ever hurt other people's feelings? If so, how?
2. Do you ever make people feel bad because of the things you say to them? If so how?
3. Do you ever make people feel bad because of what you do to them? If so, how?
4. Are people afraid of you? If so, why?
5. Would you like to be treated the way you treat others? Why or why not?
6. When you get angry, do you take it out on others? If so how?
7. Do you try to control other people by making them do things that they really don't want to do? If so how?

Do I see myself as a target?

1. Do other people ever hurt your feelings? If so how?
2. Do other people make you feel bad because of what they say to you? If so how?
3. Do other people make you feel bad because of what they do to you? If so how?
4. Are you afraid of anyone? If so why?
5. Would you like to be treated the way you treat others? If so why?
6. When others are angry, do they take their anger out on you? If so how?
7. Do other people try to control you by making you do things that you really don't want to do? If so how?

Am I a bystander?

1. Do you ever see other people get their feelings hurt? If so how?
2. Do you ever see another person feel bad because of what someone has said to them? If so, how did that make you feel?
3. Do you ever see another person feel bad because of what someone has done to them? If so, how did that make you feel?
4. Do you know anyone who causes others to be afraid of them? If so who?
5. Would you like to be treated the way you treat others? Why or why not?
6. Do you know people who take their anger out on others? If so who?
7. Do you know people who try to control other people by making them do things that they really don't want to do? If so, how does that make you feel?

Bully Beans Role Play

CAST
- Main girl in book
- Bobbette
- Main girl in book's mom
- Winston
- Teacher
- Playground Teacher
- Bystanders

- Split class into two teams.
- Using the book *Bully B.E.A.N.S.*, have each team assign cast roles.
- Practice acting out the story. Allow kids to make and use props. Use "Bully Beans" of course!
- Have teams take turns acting out role play in front of each other–have them practice giving constructive feedback. You may want to encourage healthy competition by having independent judges come in for their performances.
- Allow student teams to perform their skits in front of other grade levels and classes.
- Make sure that each team reveals a **No Tolerance for Bullying** message at the end of all performances.

How Many Bully Beans?

Fill a jar with bully (jelly) beans (counting them carefully as you put them in of course!)

Give each student a slip of paper to guess how many bully beans are in the jar. Make a bunch of extra slips and keep them handy. Each time you randomly see students being kind to one another and treating others with respect, hand them a slip so they can have another chance to guess. Keep this activity going for one week. The guess that is closest at the end of the week wins the jar of bully beans. Repeat for several weeks with different sized jars. Allow winners to share their BULLY BEANS with other students if they want to.

Power Blanket Model

To be used following Power Blanket Activity (page 3).

Doing Is Understanding!!

Materials Needed:
- 8 Standard Clothes Pins
- 1 5X8 card
- Glue (or Hot Glue Gun with Teacher's Supervision)
- Small Piece of Fabric (light colored)
- Markers

1. Decorate clothes pins into kids wearing varied colored shirts as:

    (1) Bully wears red.

    (5) Bystanders wear white.

    (2) Targets wear green.

2. Glue clothes pins side by side and evenly to the 5x8 card as shown. Make sure you put them in the right order. Let dry overnight.

3. When completely dry, trim 5x8 card so it is even with the edge of the pins.

4. Cut fabric so that it is the same length as pins.

5. Using a black permanent marker, write POWER on the fabric.

6. Grip edge of power blanket with pins.

7. Have students practice using the power blanket model, and have them take it home to show their parents.

Time to Color

Bully Board Games

> **Materials Needed:**
> - Practice paper to design a game plan
> - Markers
> - Dice
> - Poster board
> - Small items for game tokens (i.e. buttons, cotton swabs, toothpicks)
> - 3-5 cards
> - Colored paper
> - Colored craft foam
> - Paper to write the game instructions/rules on
> - Your Creativity!!!

Brainstorm as a class a list of the characteristics that bullies, targets and bystanders have. The list may include the following:

- **Bully** – rolls eyes at people, talks about others behind their back, pushes or shoves, threatens others with words, threatens others with actions, uses mean eyes, excludes certain kids from participating in activities, refuses to sit by certain kids, uses guilt to pressure others, makes fun of the way others dress, gives put-downs, spread rumors, gossips, appears to be the "teacher's pet," puts negative comments on computer communication networks, etc.

- **Target** – acts anxious, acts defensive, has an "I'm picked on" attitude, has few friends, loses interest in school, appears to be the "teacher's pet," dresses differently, may be from a different culture, ethnicity or religion, reacts to teasing, impulsive in their actions, annoys other kids and doesn't know when to stop, lacks a sense of humor, uses defeated body language (hunches, looks down instead of ahead, won't look others in the eye, backs away from others,) has little or no self-confidence, etc.

- **Strong Bystander** – cooperative, caring, assertive, not a follower, confident in his/her own abilities, careful, innovative, mediator, calm, open-minded, good sport, ability to come up with a plan or a solution to a problem and implement it, focused, genuine, goal setter and achiever, etc.

Divide students into teams of two. Have them work together to create a board games using the characteristics of the bully, the target and the bystander. **The point of each game created is to encourage bystanders to work together to take the power away from the bully, and in turn, make life for the target a little bit easier.** Have them practice drawing their game board on paper before attempting to do the final design on the poster board. Encourage them to also write an instruction card containing the rules for their game. When games are completed, have each team explain their game to the rest of the class. Allow kids to eventually try out all of the games.

Dear Bully (Inside My Head!)

Draw a detailed picture of an imaginary bully that you have inside your head.

Write a letter to your imaginary bully. In the letter, tell the bully all of the things that you don't like about him/her. Explain in detail how what they say and do is hurting others…you included! Take a stand and express to the bully that their behavior will **NO LONGER BE TOLERATED!** Give specific examples of how you plan to unplug the bully's power.

Share your letters and pictures with your class.

Bye, Bye Bully Box

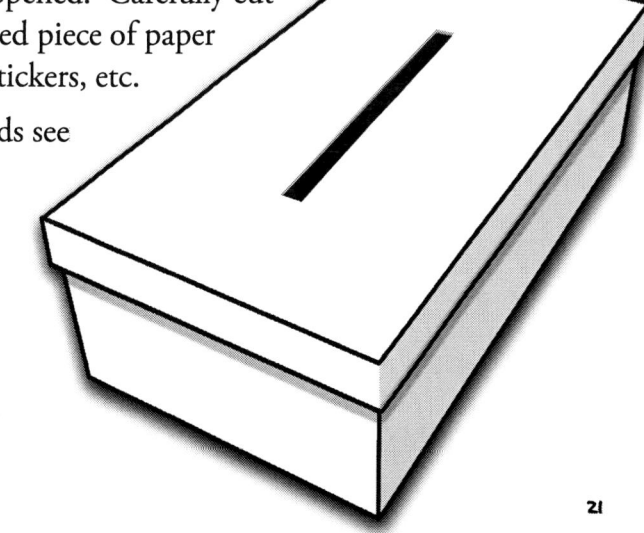

"Why don't teachers stop kids that are bullying? They do stop them when they see it happen, the problem is bullies are really sneaky and they usually don't get caught. It's always a good idea to tell a teacher or a counselor when you see bullying. If you are too scared to tell them in person, write them a note and don't sign your name."

Have students cover a shoe box with white paper, covering the lid separately so that the box can easily be opened. Carefully cut a hole in the center of the lid that is long enough for a folded piece of paper to fit through. As a class, decorate the box using markers, stickers, etc.

This box can serve as the bully reporting box. Whenever kids see any type of bullying going on, they can simply write down what is happening on a piece of paper and slip it into the box. The teacher or school counselor can read the papers periodically and take the action that is needed to unite the bystanders and stop the bullying behavior.

You Be the Author

Rewrite *Bully B.E.A.N.S.* and give it a new ending. Pretend Bobbette is a grown-up who never learned how to stop being a bully. What will happen to Bobbette? Will she have any friends? What kind of job will she have? In the box, draw a picture of Bobbette as a grown-up.

More Than Words

Our author wants you to be her new illustrator.

In each box, draw a picture that goes with the words from the story *Bully B.E.A.N.S.*

*Bobbette didn't have any real friends, but she didn't know that.
Nobody liked Bobbette, but we pretended to like her so that she wouldn't show us her mean eyes.*

*I looked Bobbette right in the eyes, but this time instead of having mean eyes,
her eyes looked scared. Her face turned white. She was in shock!*

Time to Color

"BACK OFF!"

24